Fun and Easy
Drawing

Fun and Easy Drawing
Fantasy Characters

Rosa M. Curto

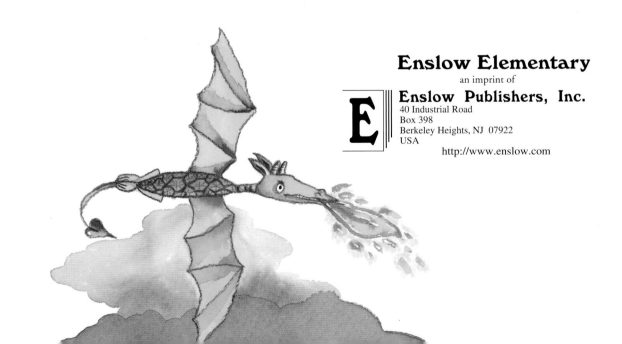

Enslow Elementary
an imprint of
Enslow Publishers, Inc.

E 40 Industrial Road
Box 398
Berkeley Heights, NJ 07922
USA

http://www.enslow.com

INTRODUCTION

Making art is a fun way to express yourself. You can create your own world and the characters that live in it! There are many different tools you can use to make art, such as markers, colored pencils, crayons, and paint. It would be best to draw in pencil first so if you make a mistake, you can erase it and try it again. Then, once you are happy with your drawing, you can color it in any way you wish.

SOME TIPS BEFORE YOU START DRAWING:

- CHOOSE A QUIET AND WELL-LIT PLACE TO WORK.

- HAVE WHAT YOU NEED TO DRAW AT HAND.

- TAKE YOUR TIME.

- HAVE FUN!

ALIENS

Draw aliens in three simple steps.

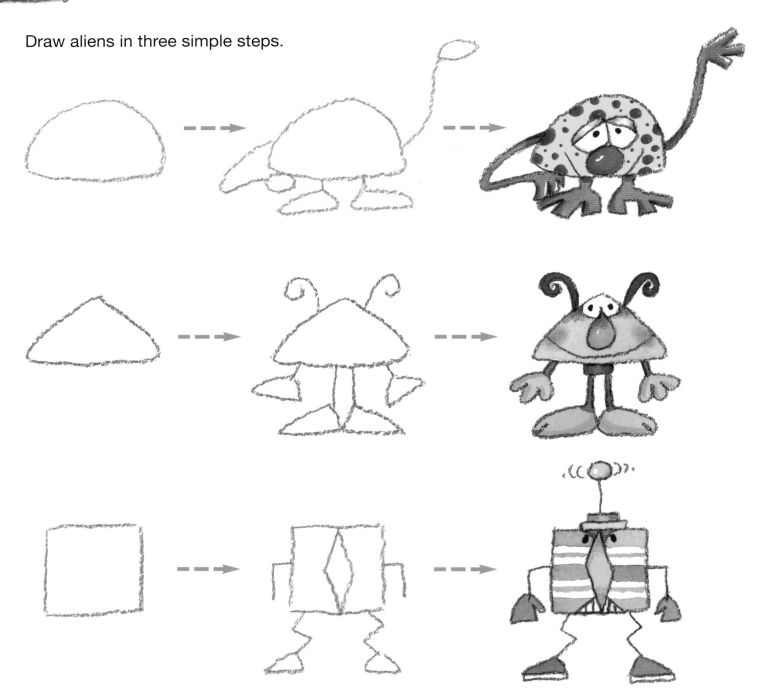

In the last step, you can color in your alien any way you like.

Create new aliens using shapes A and B.

A

B

ALIENS ARE FROM OTHER PLANETS. THEY TRAVEL IN SPACESHIPS.

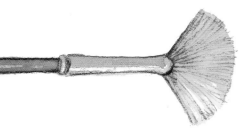

ROBOTS

Draw two rectangles.

1

Round off two sides from each rectangle.

2

3

Draw the legs.

4

Draw the antennae and the tail.

5

Draw an eye.

6

Color it in.

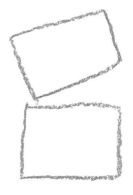

6

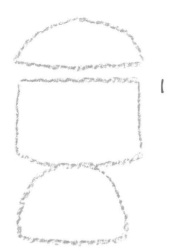

1

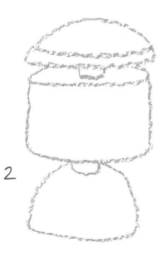

2

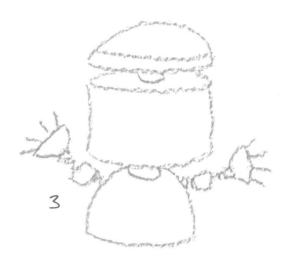

3

Draw three
simple shapes.

Join them together.

Draw the arms.

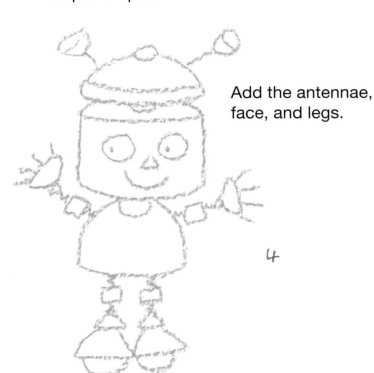

Add the antennae,
face, and legs.

4

5

Finish the details
and color it in.

A ROBOT IS A MACHINE THAT CAN DO MANY
OF THE THINGS PEOPLE CAN DO. IT CAN LOOK
LIKE A PERSON OR AN ANIMAL.

WITCH

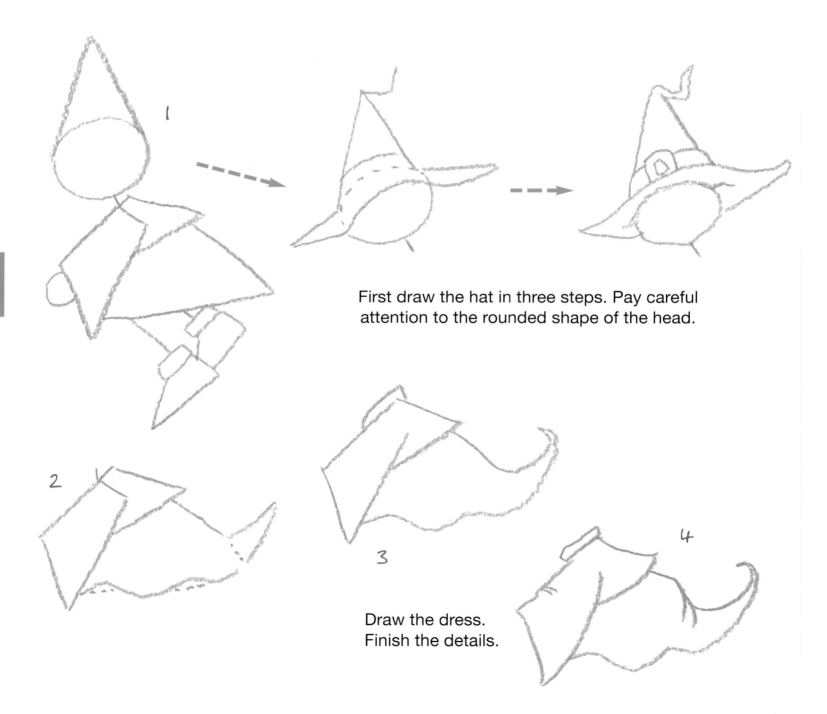

1

First draw the hat in three steps. Pay careful attention to the rounded shape of the head.

2

3

4

Draw the dress.
Finish the details.

Draw the hair, a hand, and legs.

5

Do not forget the broom!

Finish the details and color her in.

6

A WITCH CAN CAST ALL KINDS OF SPELLS. SHE CAN TURN A PRINCE INTO A FROG AND A PRINCESS INTO A SWAN.

WIZARD

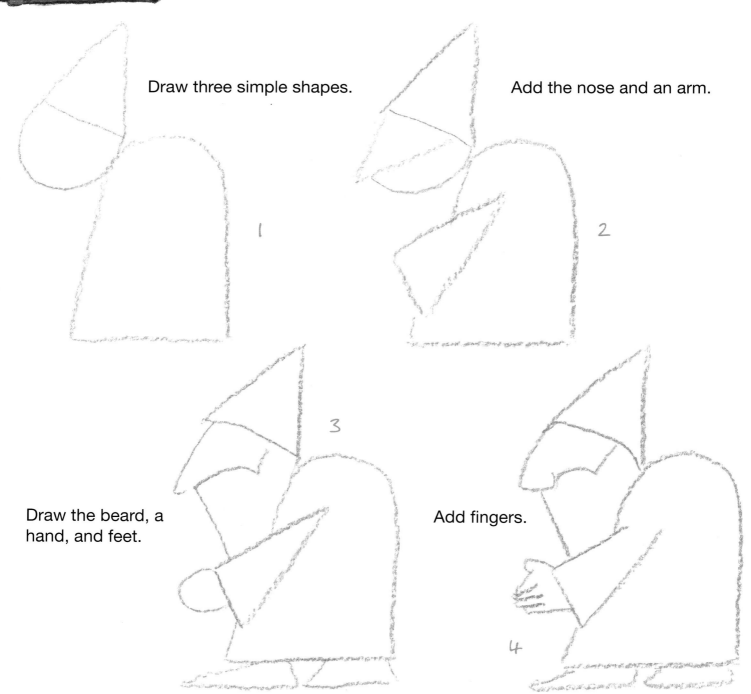

Draw three simple shapes.

1

Add the nose and an arm.

2

3

Draw the beard, a hand, and feet.

Add fingers.

4

What else can we add?

This wizard
has an owl.

5

6

7

Finish the details
and color him in.

WIZARDS HAVE
MAGICAL
POWERS JUST
LIKE WITCHES.

FAIRY

1 Draw three
simple shapes.

2 Draw an arm and legs.

3 Add the wings and
the magic wand.

4 Color her in.

You can change the color of the dress and hair.

FAIRIES LIKE TO LOOK PRETTY. THEY DECORATE
THEIR HAIR WITH FLOWERS, BERRIES, AND RIBBONS.

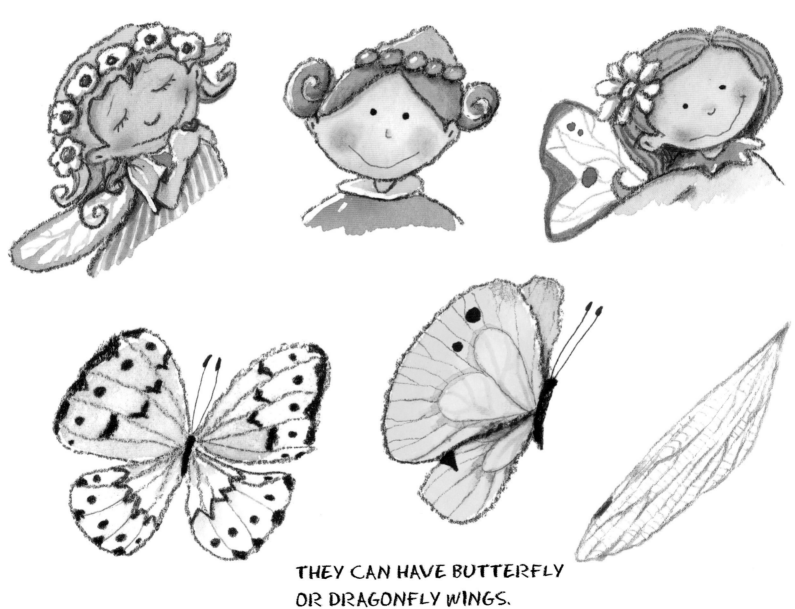

THEY CAN HAVE BUTTERFLY
OR DRAGONFLY WINGS.

ELF

1

Draw a circle and a rectangle. Add the arms and legs.

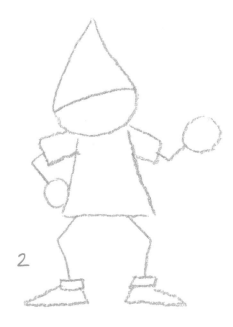

2

Draw the hat, sleeves, and shoes.

3

Draw the pants and the belt.

4

Finish the arms and legs.

5

Finish the details.

6

Color him in.

You can draw an elf in just three steps.

1

2

3

ELVES ARE VERY PLAYFUL. THEY LIKE TO HIDE PEOPLE'S THINGS.

Draw different hats.

DWARF

Draw two simple shapes.
Add arms and legs.

1

Draw the hat,
beard, and belt.

2

Add the boots and
some more details.

3

4

Draw his mustache,
sleeves, and legs.

5

6

Finish the details.

Color him in.

DWARVES LIVE
IN THE FOREST.
SOME OF THEM
WORK IN MINES.

GHOST

Draw a triangle.

1

Draw another triangle for the arm.

2

3

Add two more triangles for the nose and tail.

Round off the shapes.

4

Draw the details. Color it in.

5

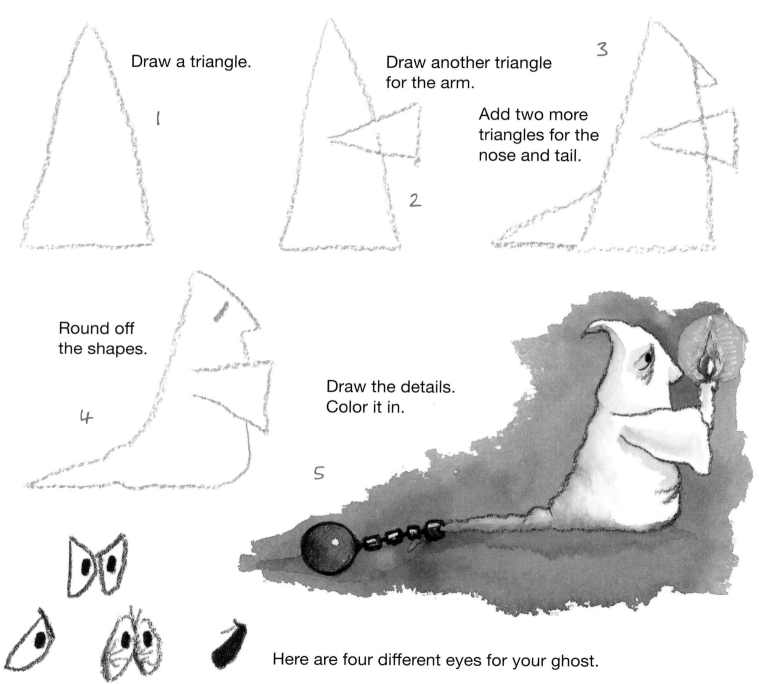

Here are four different eyes for your ghost.

Try to draw another ghost!
Start with three triangles.

1

2

How many triangles do you have now?

Round off the shapes.
Draw the eyes and mouth.

3

Add details and color it in.

4

GHOSTS WANDER AROUND AT
NIGHT SHOUTING "BOO!"

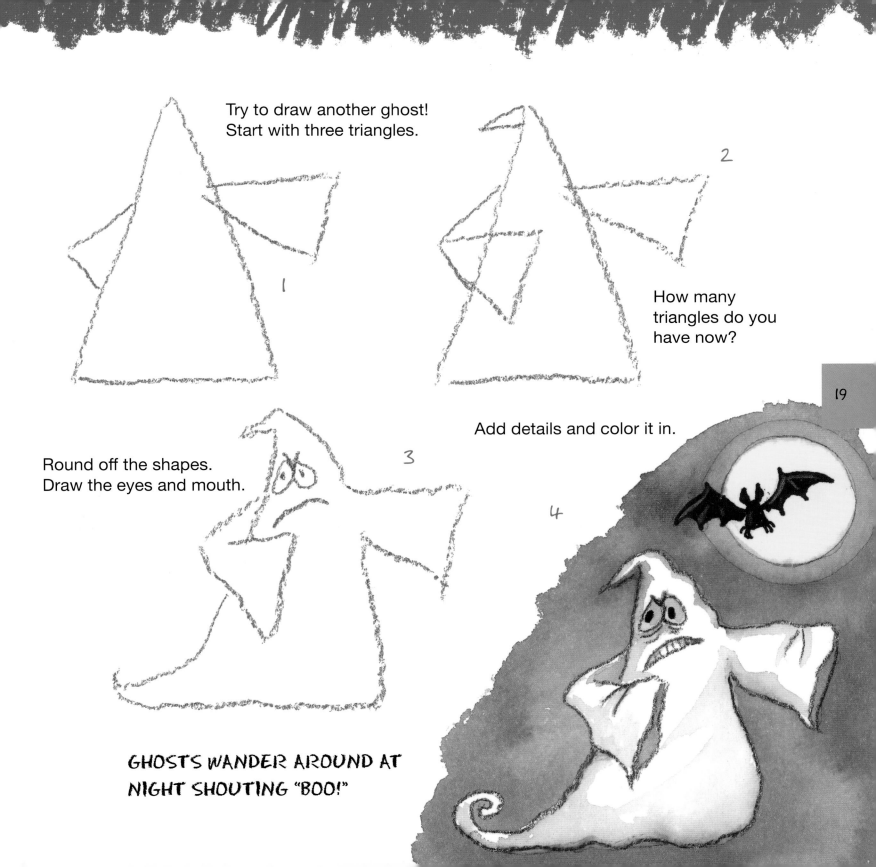

OGRE

Start with two circles.

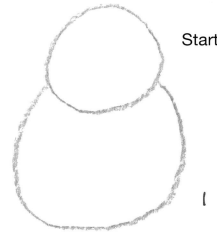

1

2

Draw the arms and legs.

Finish the arms and legs.

3

4

Draw the boots.

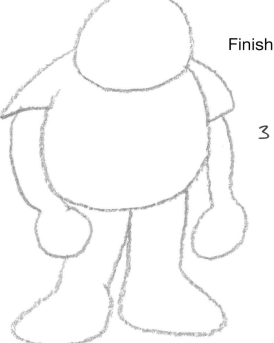

Add details.

5

Draw the face.

6

7

Finish the ogre
and color it in.

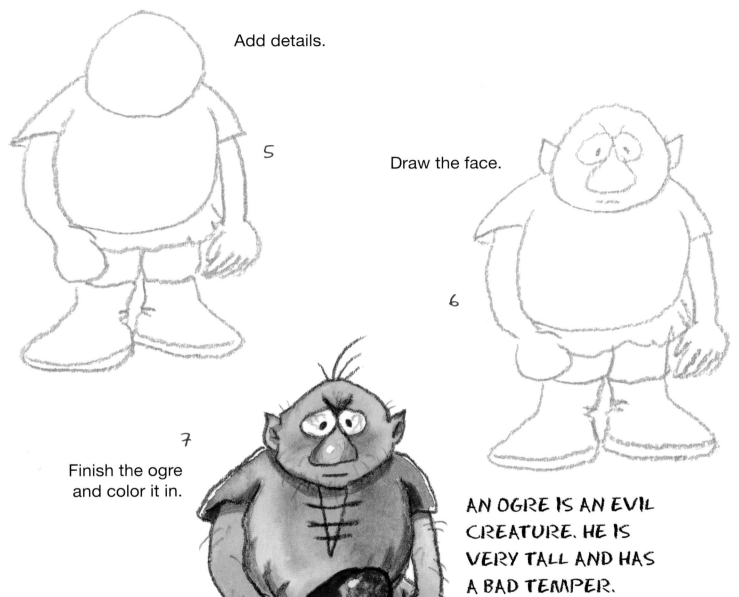

AN OGRE IS AN EVIL
CREATURE. HE IS
VERY TALL AND HAS
A BAD TEMPER.
HE ALSO SMELLS BAD!
MANY ARE GREEN,
BUT AN OGRE'S SKIN
CAN BE ANY COLOR!

WINGED HORSE

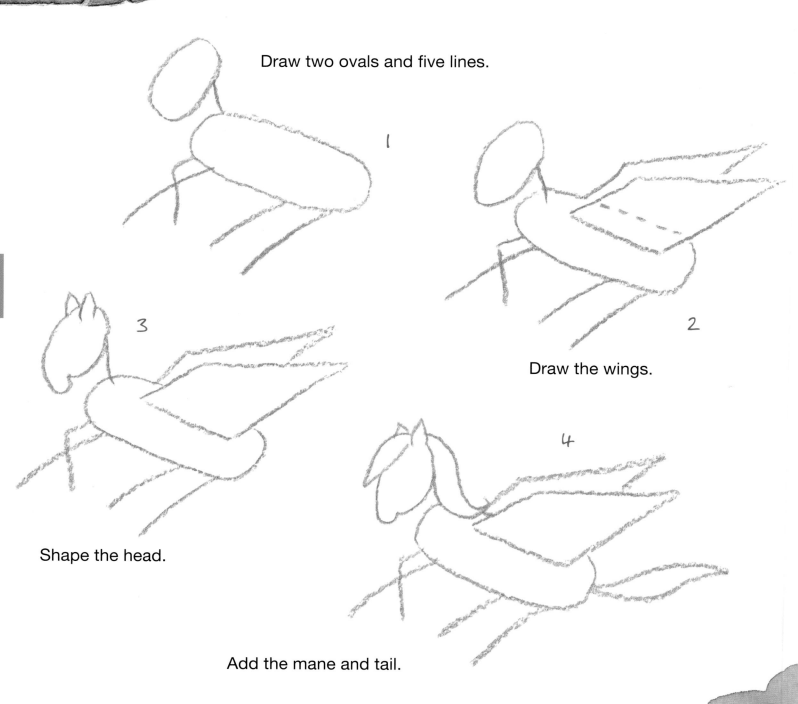

Draw two ovals and five lines.

1

2

Draw the wings.

3

Shape the head.

4

Add the mane and tail.

5

Round off the body.

6

Finish the legs.

A BEAUTIFUL WHITE
WINGED HORSE
SOARS THROUGH
THE CLOUDS!

Finish the details and
color in the horse.

7

UNICORN

Draw a triangle, a rectangle, and five lines.

Draw the legs.

Draw the neck.

Round off the body.

Draw the hooves and tail.

Draw the mane.

Finish the
details and
color it in.

A UNICORN IS AN
IMAGINARY ANIMAL.
IT LOOKS LIKE A WHITE
HORSE WITH A HORN
ON ITS FOREHEAD.

DRAGON

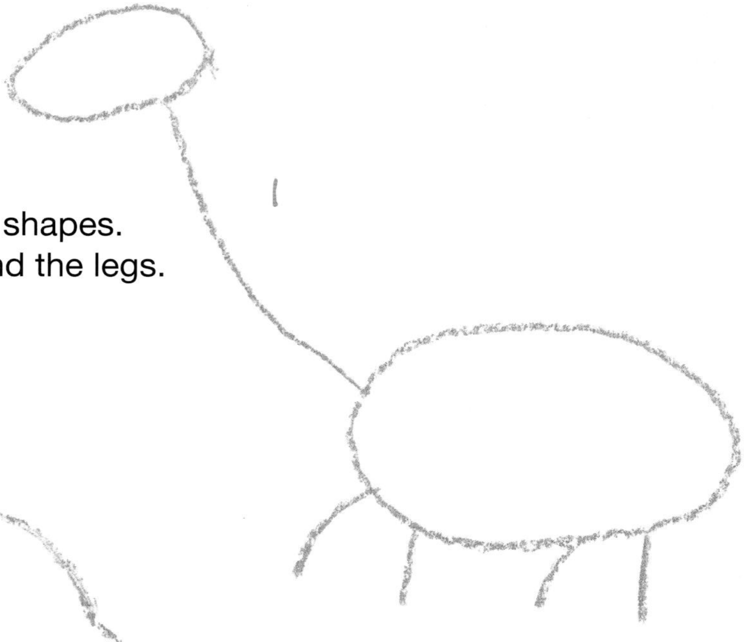

Start with two oval shapes.
Outline the neck and the legs.

1

2

Finish the neck and legs.
Draw the tail.

3

Finish the details
and color it in.

Draw a different kind of dragon. Start with three shapes: the head, body, and wings.

Mark the curves of the wings. Add the ears, horns, and legs.

Finish the details and color it in.

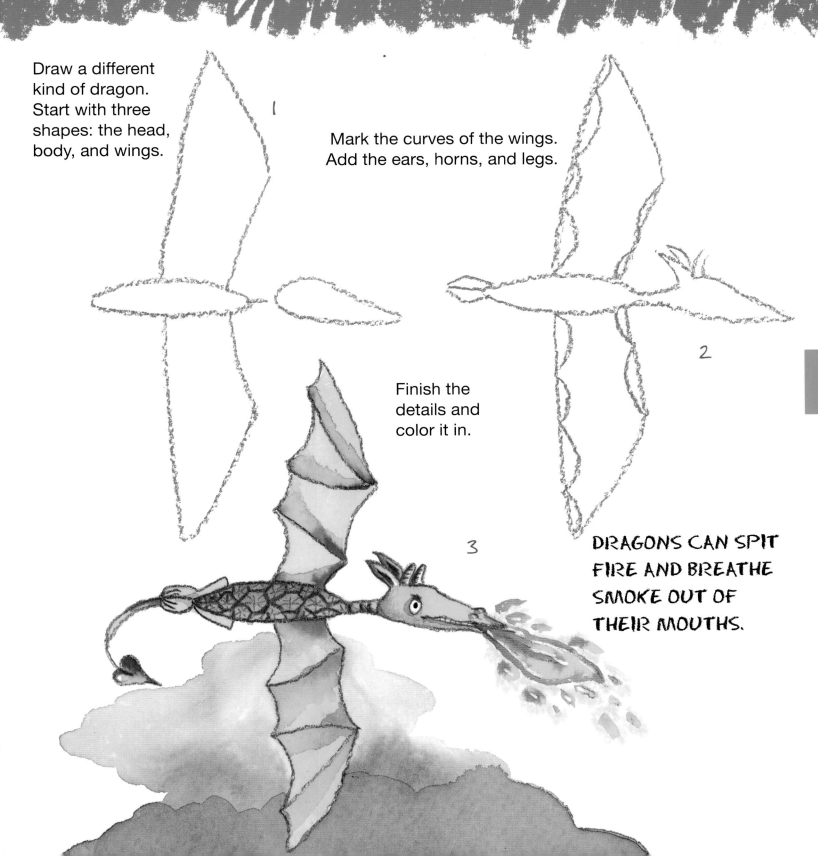

DRAGONS CAN SPIT FIRE AND BREATHE SMOKE OUT OF THEIR MOUTHS.

MERMAID

Draw a circle for the head and a rectangle for the body. Draw a fish's tail. Outline the arms and hands.

1

2

Draw the neck and her top.

3

Finish the tail.

4

Finish the arms
and draw the hands.

Do not forget her hair!

MERMAIDS HAVE FISH TAILS AND
BEAUTIFUL VOICES. SAILORS LOVE TO
HEAR THEM SING. MERMAIDS KEEP
THEIR TREASURE IN CAVES AT THE
BOTTOM OF THE SEA.

Color her in.

5

GENIE

1

Draw three shapes.

Add two lines
and the nose.

2

3

Draw the arms
and mouth.

Give him a vest.

4

Draw the eyes,
ears, and hair.

5

6

Finish the details.

7

Color him in.

A GENIE LIVES IN A
MAGIC LAMP. HE CAN
GRANT WISHES.

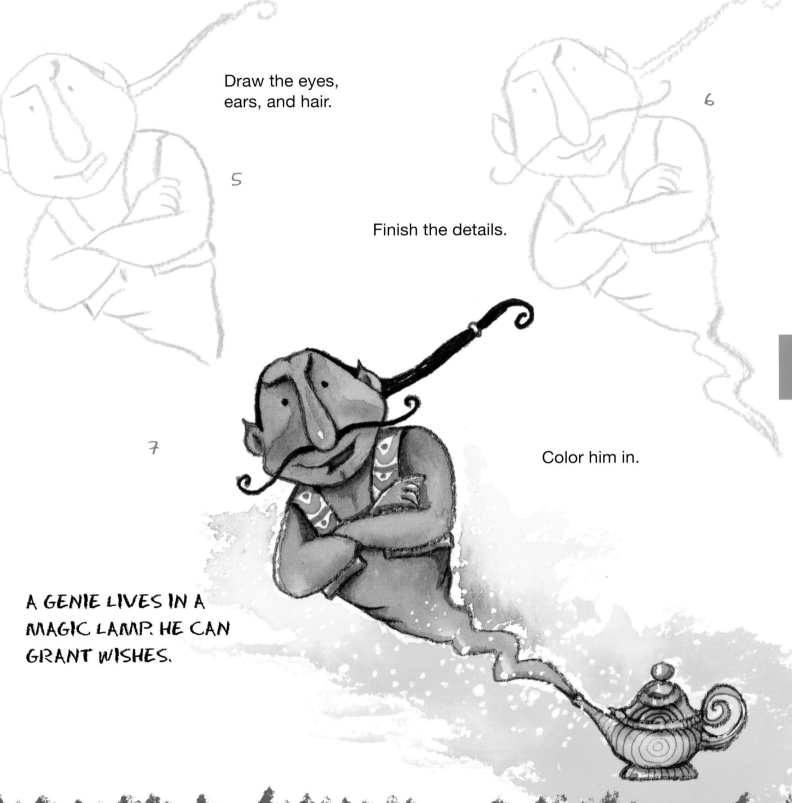

DRAWING

When you draw, you can make different types of lines:

THIN

THICK

UNEVEN

Draw the same character with a regular pencil, colored pencil, crayon, and marker. Which drawing do you like the best?

DO YOU LIKE THIS ONE?

OR THIS ONE?

You can draw lines (A) or dots (B) to make it look like there are light and shadow.

Here are two drawings.
A is normal.
B has lighter parts and darker parts.

DRAWING B LOOKS MORE INTERESTING THAN DRAWING A.

LIGHT AND SHADOW

Look at these three cubes. Each cube has one side that is lighter. Sides A, B, and C are lighter. Now you try drawing a box with a lighter side.

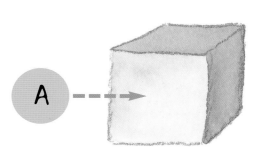

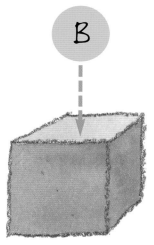

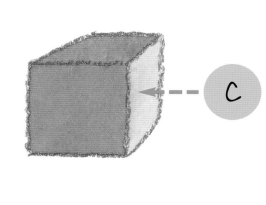

LET'S CONTINUE.
Now look at this circle. It has a point of light. If we move away from this point, the picture gets darker. The circle now looks like a ball!

Look closely at this apple. Try to draw one with light and shadow. You could also use a real apple as a model.

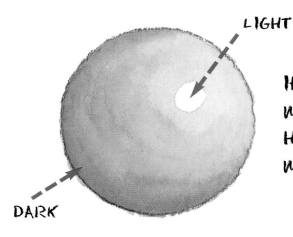

LIGHT

DARK

IF YOU SHINE A LIGHT ON A WALL AND PLACE YOUR HAND IN FRONT OF IT, YOU WILL SEE THE SHADOW.

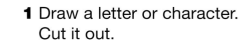

1 Draw a letter or character. Cut it out.

2 Place the image on a sheet of paper.

3 Trace it. Color the inside of the outline gray.

4 Stick the letter or character over the shadow you have just colored in. Move it down or up so it does not sit right on top of the gray shadow.

5 Add some color. Look at the result!

IT LOOKS GREAT!

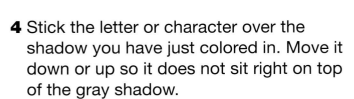

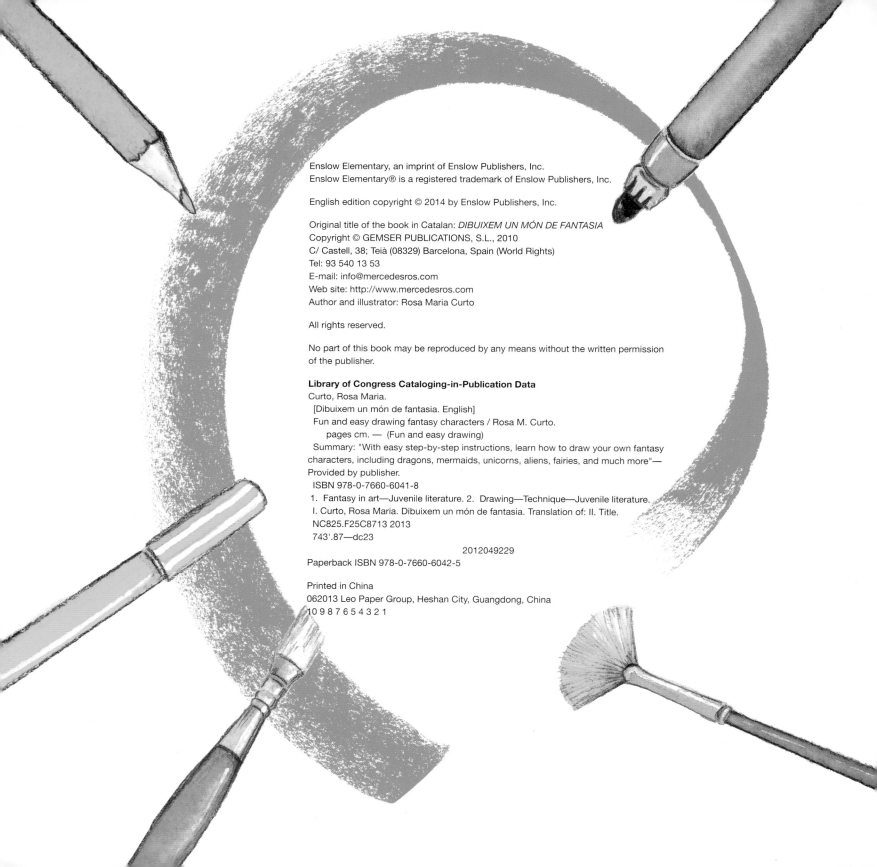

Enslow Elementary, an imprint of Enslow Publishers, Inc.
Enslow Elementary® is a registered trademark of Enslow Publishers, Inc.

Original title of the book in Catalan: *DIBUIXEM UN MÓN DE FANTASIA*
Copyright © GEMSER PUBLICATIONS, S.L., 2010
C/ Castell, 38; Teià (08329) Barcelona, Spain (World Rights)
Tel: 93 540 13 53
E-mail: info@mercedesros.com
Web site: http://www.mercedesros.com
Author and illustrator: Rosa Maria Curto

Library of Congress Cataloging-in-Publication Data
Curto, Rosa Maria.
  [Dibuixem un món de fantasia. English]
  Fun and easy drawing fantasy characters / Rosa M. Curto.
      pages cm. — (Fun and easy drawing)
  Summary: "With easy step-by-step instructions, learn how to draw your own fantasy
characters, including dragons, mermaids, unicorns, aliens, fairies, and much more"—
Provided by publisher.
  ISBN 978-0-7660-6041-8
  1. Fantasy in art—Juvenile literature. 2. Drawing—Technique—Juvenile literature.
  I. Curto, Rosa Maria. Dibuixem un món de fantasia. Translation of: II. Title.
  NC825.F25C8713 2013
  743'.87—dc23
                                    2012049229
Paperback ISBN 978-0-7660-6042-5

Printed in China
062013 Leo Paper Group, Heshan City, Guangdong, China
10 9 8 7 6 5 4 3 2 1